I have only

told the half

of what I saw.

— MARCO POLO

The Adventures of MARCO POLO

by RUSSELL FREEDMAN

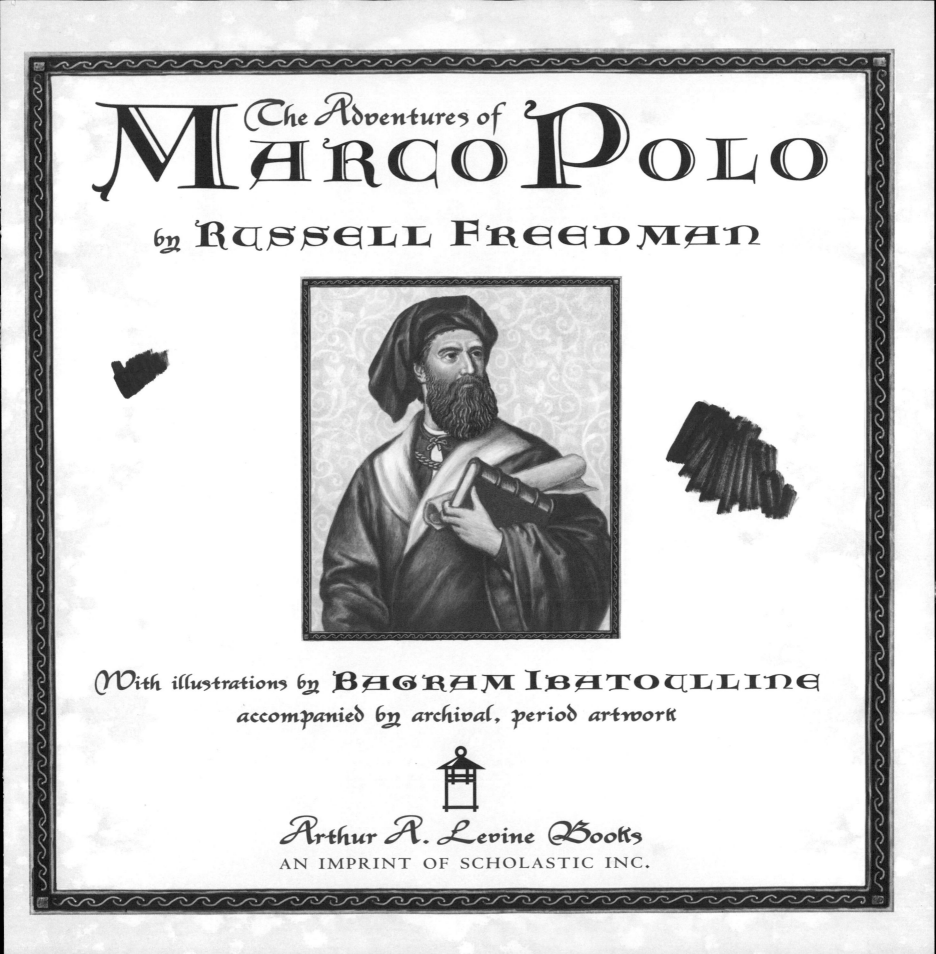

With illustrations by BAGRAM IBATOULLINE

accompanied by archival, period artwork

Arthur A. Levine Books

AN IMPRINT OF SCHOLASTIC INC.

To "Aunt Betty,"
an explorer of the heart — R. F.

To the Liberman family with love — B. I.

The publisher gratefully acknowledges the following people for their expert advice: Marc Aronson;
Consuelo W. Dutschke, Ph.D., curator of Medieval and Renaissance Manuscripts at Columbia University's Rare Book and Manuscript Library;
and Morris Rossabi, professor of Inner Asian and East Asian history at Columbia University.

Library of Congress Cataloging-in-Publication Data

Freedman, Russell.
The Adventures of Marco Polo / by Russell Freedman ; illustrated by Bagram Ibatoulline. — 1st American ed.
p. cm.
ISBN 0-439-52394-X
1. Polo, Marco, 1254-1323?—Pictorial works. 2. Explorers—Italy—Biography—Pictorial works.
3. Storytelling—Pictorial works. 4. Travel, Medieval—Pictorial works. 5. Asia—Description and travel—Pictorial works.
I. Title.   G370.P9F74 2006   910.4—dc22   2005022791

10 9 8 7 6 5 4 3 2 1   06 07 08 09 10

Book design by Elizabeth B. Parisi
Photo research by Amla Sanghvi and Rachel Griffiths

First edition, October 2006
Printed in Singapore   46

CONTENTS

Nothing But the Truth

As Marco Polo lay dying, friends and relatives gathered anxiously by his bedside and begged him to confess. They pleaded with him to tell the truth, to renounce his exaggerations and lies, so he might meet his maker with a clear conscience.

He was known in some circles as "the man of a million lies." And all because of a book in which he told fantastic tales about his travels and adventures.

In an age when the Earth was said to be flat, Marco claimed that he had visited a distant and unknown land so far away, so difficult to reach, that no European had been there before and come back to tell the tale. According to his book, he had traveled thousands of miles with his father and uncle by donkey, horse, and camel, braving bandits and man-eating beasts, crossing barren deserts where the sands at night cry like lost men, scaling mountain passes at the roof of the world where no birds fly "because of the height and the cold."

After a journey lasting three and a half years, Marco wrote, the Polos arrived at the dazzling court of Kublai Khan, conquerer of China and the world's most powerful ruler. From his marble palace, "the largest ever seen," the Great Khan reigned over a vast empire of thriving cities and towns, far richer in goods, services, and technology than any place in Europe.

Marco told his readers that he became a trusted envoy of the Khan's, who sent him on confidential missions to every part of the empire. His travels took him to "a greater number of different regions in that part of the world than any man who was ever born."

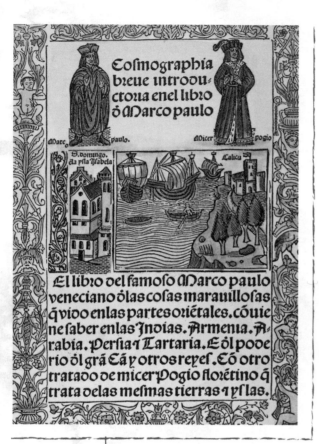

His book chronicled things that seemed so amazing, many readers refused to believe him: rocks that burned and pieces of paper as valuable as gold; "black lions" and "snakes with legs"; bandits who turned day to night, people who decorated their bodies with ink, sorcerers who hypnotized sharks, and a king who had 500 wives.

After spending many years in China and the lands beyond, Marco made his way back to Venice, his hometown. One more adventure awaited him. Soon after he returned, he was captured during a sea battle between Venice and Genoa, rival city states that were fighting for control of the Mediterranean. It seems that Marco, an experienced seaman, had been put in command of a Venetian war galley. When the Venetians went down in defeat, he wound up as a prisoner of war in Genoa, where he was held for a year or so until the city states signed a peace treaty in 1299.

Marco shared his prison cell with a fellow named Rustichello of Pisa, who had been captured in an earlier sea battle between Pisa and Genoa. Now it happened that Rustichello was a writer, the author of epic romances about the days of chivalry. His books, like all books in Europe before the introduction of printing, had to be transcribed — copy after copy — by hand. They could be found in the libraries of certain princes and lords, along with finely bound and illustrated works of religion and philosophy. Ordinary folk heard his stories when professional storytellers recited them in the marketplace.

It isn't hard to imagine the gleam of interest in Rustichello's eyes as he listened to Marco's travel tales, which seemed far more adventurous than any story Rustichello himself had ever imagined. And so the practiced writer of romances teamed up with the restless wanderer. Marco sent to Venice for his travel notes and began to dictate an account of his adventures to Rustichello. The book that resulted carried the bold title, *The Description of the World*.

After his release from prison, Marco settled down as a merchant in Venice, where he lived quietly. Handwritten copies of his book, meanwhile, circulated throughout Italy, and the book was translated into several European languages. *The Description of the World* opened the eyes of Europeans to a civilization they had known almost nothing about, and it fired the imaginations of explorers like Christopher Columbus. But many readers continued to regard the book as a fantastic collection of tall tales.

Skeptics scoffed at Marco's stories. They dismissed him as a liar and a charlatan. Even today, seven centuries later, the truth of Marco Polo's book is still being debated. Did he really travel to China and beyond, as he claimed? Or was he, in fact, "the man of a million lies"?

To his dying day, Marco insisted that he was telling the truth. "Read through this book," says the prologue, "and you will find all kinds of wonderful things . . . as they were related by Marco Polo, a wise and noble citizen of Venice, who states distinctly those things he saw with his own eyes, and those he heard about from others. And we shall set down things seen as seen, and things heard as heard only, so that those who read our book, or hear it read to them, may have full faith that it contains nothing but the truth."

The Polo Brothers

Venice rose from the sea at the center of the world—or so it must have seemed to a boy growing up there in the 13th century. Tall-masted sailing ships from distant ports tied up at Venice's busy wharves, and the streets were thronged with traders and sailors speaking many languages. The city's influence reached across the Mediterranean to the Black Sea, where Venetian merchants grew rich dealing in precious goods brought by camel caravan from faraway kingdoms to the East.

Marco Polo's father, Niccolò, and his uncle, Maffeo, were partners in a family trading company. Around 1260, when Marco was six, the Polo brothers set out from their base on the Black Sea with trunks full of jewels to trade at the court of a wealthy ruler in western Russia. They would be gone for nine years, much longer than anyone had expected.

Marco's mother died while his father and uncle were away, and the boy was raised by relatives. He grew up in the parish of San Severo, a bustling district of narrow lanes, unpaved footpaths, and canals that led to the breathtaking expanse of St. Mark's Square, at the heart of the city. Money changers, food vendors, and merchants of every kind hawked their wares in the great square. Knights jousted there and criminals were displayed in a cage suspended from the tall bell tower, where every passerby could stop to jeer at them. In bed at night, Marco could hear the tower's bell tolling the hours.

As the son of a merchant, Marco was destined to follow in his father's footsteps. His student

workbooks were filled with tips on business, taxes, and fees; notes on the conversion of foreign money, weights, and measures into Venetian money, weights, and measures; and practical mathematical problems designed to prepare a boy for a lifetime of mental calculations.

The workbooks also offered wise sayings ("Courtesy from the mouth is very valuable and costs little"); religious prayers and charms ("When you want to go on board a ship, recommend yourself to Saint Oriele and Tobias"); and advice on predicting the weather ("Know that if the sun will be very pale in the morning, that is, lifeless in color as if bleached, or yellowish, it means that there will be storms that day").

Marco was fifteen when his father and uncle finally returned to Venice. And he listened in amazement as Niccolò and Maffeo told of their adventures. Drawn by chance, by accidents of trade and war, they had traveled farther to the East than any westerners before them.

After trading their jewels in western Russia, the brothers found that their way home was blocked by a war that had broken out between rival rulers in the region. To steer clear of the fighting, they made a wide detour and found refuge in Bukhara (now in Uzbekistan), which

they described as "the finest city in all of Persia." There they were stranded for three years as they waited for the fighting to end.

The brothers were rescued when a Mongol envoy passing through the city invited them to join a diplomatic mission on its way to the court of Kublai Khan, ruler of the Mongol Empire, who "lived at the ends of the earth in an east-northerly direction." The Khan would be pleased to speak with them, the envoy said, for he had

Niccolò and Maffeo Polo before the Great Khan, from the Livre des Merveilles du Monde, a 15th-century French edition of Marco Polo's book. One of the few surviving and most highly regarded illuminated manuscripts of his travels.

never met any person from their part of the world. The Polos, in turn, knew almost nothing about the Great Khan and *his* part of the world.

Mongol armies had recently conquered northern China, known to Europeans as Cathay, and had overrun most of central Asia and Russia. Moving with lightning speed, Mongol warriors wearing leather and steel had galloped west into Europe, penetrating as far as Germany and Hungary. With their deadly archery and sure mastery of horse power, they had spread terror and panic before withdrawing back to their stronghold on the grassy Asian steppes.

Rumors concerning these Mongols had multiplied like fevers during an epidemic. It was said that Mongol horsemen could ride ten days and nights without stopping to make a fire or heat food, sleeping in the saddle and living only on blood from cuts they made in their horses' backs. "The men are inhuman and of the nature of beasts, rather to be called monsters than men, thirsting after and drinking blood, and tearing and devouring the flesh of dogs and human beings," warned Matthew Paris, a Benedictine monk at an abbey in England.

And yet, Niccolò and Maffeo found their Mongol hosts to be nothing like the barbarians described in European stories. In Bukhara, they were assured safe-conduct if they joined the diplomatic mission to the Great Khan's court. Stranded with no prospect of returning home anytime soon, they agreed to set out with the Mongol envoy and his party. According to

A 13th-century Persian miniature of Mongol warriors attacking a citadel. At its height, the Mongol Empire stretched well into Europe and the Middle East.

A golden paiza,
or passport,
from the
Mongolian Empire
(1206-1368).

Marco, they traveled for a whole year toward the north and northeast, passing through many countries and venturing farther than any westerners before them, beyond Mongolia to the palace of Kublai Khan in the heart of Cathay.

As promised, the Khan welcomed them. He asked many questions about the land they came from and about their Christian faith, and he listened with interest to all they had to tell.

Pleased with what he had heard, Kublai made up his mind to send emissaries to the Roman Catholic Pope, Clement IV, and he asked Niccolò and Maffeo to undertake this mission for him. He invited the Pope to send him "a hundred men learned in the Christian religion" and well-versed in western knowledge. And he asked for some oil from the lamp that burned at the Church of the Holy Sepulchre (the tomb of Jesus) in Jerusalem, considered a balm for body and soul.

When the brothers were ready to leave, the Khan gave them a *paiza*, an inscribed gold tablet the size of a man's hand that served as a VIP passport, guaranteeing the travelers safe passage. It commanded officials throughout the Khan's domains to provide the brothers with horses, lodging, food, and escorts as they made their way back to Europe. Marco tells us that it took them fully three years to return home: "It took so long because they could not always proceed, being stopped sometimes by snow or by heavy rains falling, or by great torrents which they found in an impassible state."

The Polos departing Venice, from perhaps the most famous surviving Marco Polo illuminated manuscript, a 15th-century English book currently at Oxford's Bodleian Library.

The Polos returned to Venice in 1269, but by then, Pope Clement IV had died. They waited for two years until a new pope, Gregory X, was elected. Then they set off once again for the East. This time, Marco went with them. He was now an energetic youth of seventeen.

They sailed south down the Adriatic, around the southern tip of Greece, and across the Mediterranean to the Holy Land, where Pope Gregory was staying at the time. He gave the Polos his blessing and allowed them to obtain a vial of holy oil from the lamp burning in Jerusalem. But instead of a hundred learned men, as Kublai Khan had requested, the Pope appointed just two Dominican friars to accompany the Polos, men "who were assuredly the wisest in all that province." He entrusted the friars with valuable gifts and a friendly letter to deliver to the Khan.

From the Holy Land, the Polos and the friars sailed to the Mediterranean port of Layas (also known as Ayas or Lajazzo), a busy jumping-off place for travelers going eastward. There they joined a caravan of armed merchants who traveled together for protection against bandits. Loading their goods on huge two-wheeled wooden carts pulled by donkeys, they set out on horseback, saddlebags bouncing and rattling, horses snorting and wheezing, covering perhaps twenty-five miles a day as they rode across Turkey and into Persia (present-day Iran).

But the friars found the journey far more difficult than they had expected. They soon made their excuses, handed over their credentials, the gifts, and the Pope's letter, and turned back, leaving Niccolò, Maffeo, and Marco on the road.

As Marco tells the story, the Polos pressed on without them.

The Road to Cathay

The lands of what are now Turkey and Iran were familiar territory to Italian merchants. But to Marco, who had never traveled far from Venice, every mile brought new sights and experiences.

The Polos' caravan passed through busy cities where minarets soared above golden mosques and merchants haggled in overflowing bazaars. In the countryside, they met wandering shepherds who carried their houses on horseback. "They live entirely off their flocks," wrote Marco, "and have clothing of animal skins and tents made of skins or felt."

Farther east, near the Caspian Sea, Marco was astonished to see a fountain of oil gushing from the ground as though from a spring. "This oil is not good to eat [like olive oil]," he noted, "but is good for burning and is also used as an ointment to cure itches and scabs in men and camels. People come from long distances to fetch it, and in the surrounding country, no other oil is used in their lamps." Marco was probably the first European to describe a source of petroleum.

Riding past fortified castles and walled towns, creeping along twisting mountain roads, their caravan arrived at Tabriz, "a large and very noble city" in Persia, and an important crossroads. From there, the Polos headed south, spending day after sweaty day in the saddle as they crossed a sun-baked plateau where "the wells and other watering places lie so far apart, you must travel long distances before your horses and pack mules have anything to drink."

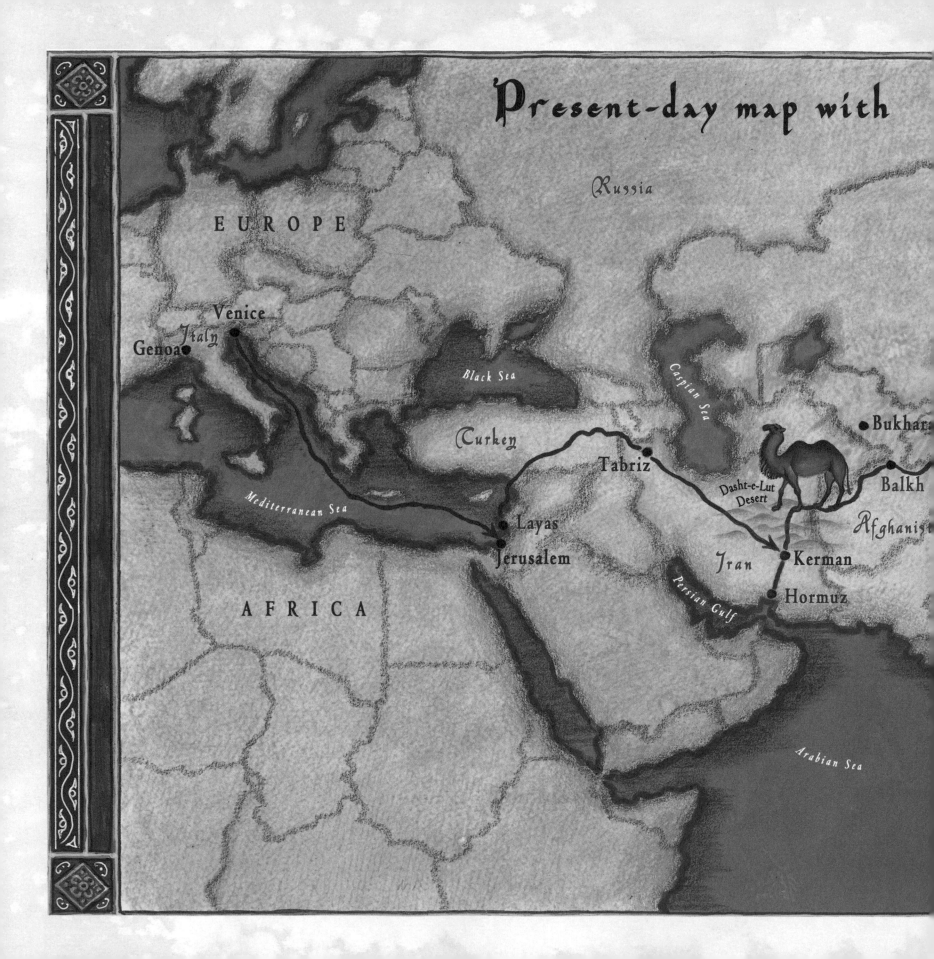

Present-day map with

EUROPE

Russia

Venice

Genoa Italy

Black Sea

Caspian Sea

Turkey

Tabriz

Bukhara

Mediterranean Sea

Dasht-e-Lut
Desert

Balkh

Layas

Jerusalem

Iran

Kerman

Afghanist

AFRICA

Persian Gulf

Hormuz

Arabian Sea

Marco Polo's route to Kublai Khan

(13th-century names in red)

Mongolia

Gobi Desert

Shangdu

Daidu

amirs

Kashgar

Taklimakan Desert

Kunlun

ASIA

Yellow River

ndu Kush

Himalayas

China

Quinsai

Yangtze River

Yunnan

India

Mekong River

Bay of Bengal

Pacific Ocean

At length they reached the Persian Gulf and the steamy port of Hormuz. "Traders come here by ship from all parts of India," wrote Marco, "bringing spices and drugs, precious stones and pearls, fabrics of silk and gold, elephants' tusks, and many other wares."

At Hormuz, the Polos planned to find a ship that would take them to India. From there, they hoped, they could sail to the coast of China. But when they saw the poor condition of the vessels at Hormuz, they changed their plans: "Their ships are wretched affairs, and many of them get lost, because they are not fastened together with iron nails. Instead, the hulls are stitched together with twine made of coconut fibers. This makes it a risky business to sail in these ships. And you can take my word that many of them sink, because in the Indian Ocean, the storms are often terrible."

They decided to backtrack and continue their journey by land. So the saddle-sore travelers rode north again as far as the city of Kerman, then turned eastward toward the rising sun. All along, they had to watch for bandits who prowled the countryside, stalking caravans and hunting down stragglers. "Unless the merchants in the caravans are well-armed and equipped with bows, bandits will rob and slay them without mercy," Marco warned.

In eastern Persia, the Polos and their fellow travelers traded their horses for camels, which were better suited to make the long trip across the sand and stone desert that lay ahead—

A camel caravan. A detail from the Catalan Atlas (c. 1375), a medieval master map highly influenced by Marco Polo's account of his travels.

the Dasht-e-Lut, the Desert of Emptiness. Camels and pack mules had to be loaded with goatskins filled with water and with enough food to last at least eight days. For long stretches during the desert crossing, "there are no towns or villages," wrote Marco. "It is all a desolate and arid waste. There are no animals at all, because they could find nothing to eat. A traveler has to carry with him all that he needs to eat or drink."

With no trace of vegetation in sight, they built glowing campfires of dry camel dung at night and ate their evening meal under the stars as the hobbled camels, grunting and grumbling, grazed nearby. In the confusion of the frosty dawn, after striking their tents, the drivers held the camels' necks to the ground while the baggage packs were being fastened to their backs, the great beasts struggling and groaning and roaring, the drivers kicking and cursing.

While making their way across this desert, the Polos' caravan was caught in a blinding sandstorm. Winds whipped and howled, kicking up clouds of sand and dust, turning the day as dark as night, making it impossible to see more than a few feet ahead. As sand swirled around the caravan, bandits galloped out of the darkness.

Marco had been told that the darkness was brought about by a spell conjured up by the bandits, a robber tribe known as the Caraunas: "When these robbers wish to raid and plunder, they cast a devilish spell, so that the day turns dark, and you can scarcely see your comrade riding beside you . . . when they have brought on the darkness, they ride side by side, sometimes thousands of them, and attack. Nothing they find in the open country, man, woman, or beast, can escape them. When they have taken captives who cannot pay a ransom, they kill the old folk, and the young men and women they lead away and sell as serfs and slaves."

The Caraunas probably did not cast a spell, as Marco may have believed, but were shrewd enough to lie in wait and attack during a sandstorm. When they appeared without warning, the travelers and their camels scattered. The three Polos narrowly evaded capture, escaping to the safety of a village. But others in the caravan "were caught and sold, and some were put to death," according to Marco, who devotes only two sentences in his book to what must have been a terrifying experience.

Moving on, the Polos passed from Persia into Afghanistan. They were now following the southern branch of the Silk Road, the ancient caravan trail that linked the Chinese East to the Muslim West. As far back as the Roman Empire, long caravans of camels had traveled this perilous route, carrying great quantities of Chinese silk to the West, and returning East with cargoes of gold, gemstones, perfumes, pomegranates, and other precious goods, including music, knowledge, and novel ideas.

Along the way they passed the ruins of Balkh, once one of the world's great cities, which had been sacked and ravaged a half-century earlier by the Mongol warriors of Genghis Khan. "I can tell you that there used to be many fine palaces and mansions of marble, which can still be seen, but they are shattered now and in ruins," Marco reported. The desolate palaces were now dwelling places for ravens and screech owls which answered one another's cries, while in the empty halls the winds moaned.

As they approached the foothills of the Pamir Mountains in northern Afghanistan, Marco fell ill, from malaria perhaps. He recuperated, he tells us, by going up into the mountains, "where the air is so pure and healthy, that when people who live below in the valleys and towns fall sick or come down with a fever, they lose no time in climbing into the mountains, where a few days' rest restores them to health."

When Marco recovered, the Polos went on their way. The trail, padded soft by centuries of camels, wound around precipitous ledges through narrow, high-walled valleys and followed a rushing stream that led them higher and higher toward lofty snowcapped peaks. The pack mules scampered and clattered up jagged hillsides. The camels leaped from rock to rock, while the wind whistled across every ridge and whined through the canyons. They were now in the high Pamir, which the local people called the "Roof of the World." Ahead of them rose the towering mountains of the Hindu Kush, "said to be the highest place in the world," wrote Marco.

On the other side lay the city of Kashgar in what is today China, a distance of 250 miles as the crow flies. But trudging along steep narrow trails with their animals and belongings, waiting out sudden blizzards, fording swollen rivers, making detours around avalanches, the Polos needed nearly two months to cross the mountains.

The trail they followed topped 15,000 feet. "No birds fly here because of the height and the cold," Marco reported. He noticed that "fire does not burn so brightly, nor give out as much heat as usual, and food does not cook as well." He believed that the weak flames were due to "this great cold." Actually, the flames were weak because of the oxygen-thin air at that altitude.

This 19th-century image of camels in the dunes of Central Asia shows a scene virtually unchanged from Marco Polo's time.

On the other side of the mountains, the trail dropped down to a chilly and treeless plain. They moved on to the oasis city of Kashgar, an ancient trading center along the Silk Road with its fine gardens, orchards, and vineyards. There they replenished their supplies in open-air markets where merchants wearing silk turbans sold splendid rugs and bartered for horses.

Now they faced the most perilous part of their journey. They were about to cross the windswept Taklimakan Desert, known as "the Sea of Death," and even today considered a forbidding place. As the local people in those days warned, "Go in and you won't come out." At the edge of the desert, which is roughly the size of modern Germany, was a town called Lop (present-day Charkhlik), where the Polos stopped for a week to refresh themselves and their animals and stock up on provisions.

They planned to cross at the desert's narrowest point, a trip that would take a month. Along the way they would find a few small oases, islands of trees and greenery fed by ancient irrigation channels that brought snow water from the distant Kunlun mountain range. But as their camels plodded along, the oases became scarce, and the sand dunes rose mountain high.

"You must go for a day and a night before you find fresh water," Marco reported. "There are no birds or beasts because there is nothing for them to eat."

Though the desert seemed lifeless, the travelers heard weird lifelike sounds. "The truth is this," wrote Marco. "When travelers are on the move at night, and one of them happens to lag behind, or falls asleep, and loses touch with his companions, afterwards, when he wants to rejoin them, he hears spirits talking to him as if they are his companions. Sometimes the spirits will call him by name, and make him stray from the path, so that he never finds it again. And in this way, many travelers have been lost and have perished. . . . Yes, and even by daylight travelers may hear these spirit voices, and often they hear the sounds of musical instruments, especially drums, and the clash of arms.

"For this reason," Marco continued, "travelers make a point of staying very close together. They set up a sign pointing in the direction of the next day's travel before they go to sleep. And round the necks of their camels and pack animals they fasten little bells, so that by listening to the sound, they may prevent them from straying off the path."

Those ghostly voices can still be heard today in the Taklimakan. Modern travelers say that the sounds are produced by shifting sands, or by the moaning of winds blowing across the dunes. But some folks living there insist that the sounds come from the wailing of evil spirits.

As the Polos emerged safely from the dreaded desert, they were entering a world that few Europeans had seen. For the first time, Marco found himself among large numbers of Chinese, along with Mongols, Tibetans, Turks, and others, peoples who spoke several languages and practiced different religions. Following the Silk Road, they met Buddhists, Muslims, and Christians, and saw monasteries, abbeys, and temples with golden statues of

Buddha and monks clad in saffron robes. They still had mountains and deserts to cross, but now they were deep in the realm of Kublai Khan, and every step brought them closer to the legendary cities of the Chinese East.

When word of their approach reached the mighty ruler, he sent couriers out to meet them and escort them to his summer capital at Shangdu (also known as Xanadu), which was still forty days' distant. Marco tells us that they arrived at Shangdu in the spring of 1275, three and a half years after they had set out from Venice. With their detours, they had traveled perhaps 8,000 miles before reaching their destination in China. And the Great Khan was waiting for them.

The story of the Polos' arrival at the court of Kublai Khan captured the imagination of readers for centuries. This 1901 illustration is from an American book.

In the Court of Kublai Khan

Shangdu stood in a wide valley, where it could "be seen from very far away." As the Polos approached the city, the glazed roof tiles of palaces and temples, "scarlet and green and blue and yellow," gleamed brightly in the morning sunlight.

To Europeans who feared the Mongols as rude barbarians, Marco's description of Kublai Khan's luxurious court seemed an impossible dream. Entering the city wall, the Polos were ushered into "a vast marble palace." They were led down long ornate hallways, through flowered courtyards and gilded chambers "decorated with handsome paintings of men and beasts and birds." Hundreds of silk-robed servants and officials watched silently and bowed as the foreign visitors filed past. Finally they were escorted into the royal chamber, where the Great Khan of the Mongols sat on his throne with his tame lion at his feet. Marco and his father and his uncle fell to their knees before the sovereign and bowed deeply, beating their heads upon the carpeted floor.

The Khan motioned for them to rise. This mighty ruler was now a stout fellow of sixty years with a wispy beard, a ruddy complexion, and "black and handsome eyes." He welcomed the Polos to his court and asked about their journey, the countries they had seen, and how they had fared. They presented him with the letters and gifts the Pope had sent, and with the holy oil, "which the Khan received with joy and prized very highly."

Turning to Marco, the Khan asked, "And who is he?"

"Sire," Niccolò replied, "he is my son, and your loyal subject."

"Then he is welcome, too," said the Khan.

"What need to make a long story of it?" wrote Marco. "Great indeed were the mirth and merrymaking with which the Great Khan and all his court welcomed these emissaries."

Kublai Khan was the grandson

A 14th-century depiction of Genghis Khan from Persia, where the Mongols controlled vast lands. The military prowess of Mongol warriors left Kublai Khan with a massive empire at his command.

of Genghis Khan, the fearless Mongol chieftain whose armies had swept across a continent. By the time the Polos arrived in Shangdu, the Mongol Empire, stretching from what is now China to Russia and Iraq, was at its height. Marco described Kublai as "the most powerful ruler, in subjects and in land and in treasure, that the world has ever known."

The Khan's palace stood at the entrance to a park where deer grazed in lush meadows and drank from playing fountains. In the middle of the park, within a grove of trees, was an enormous collapsible building, a royal pavilion for parties and banquets constructed entirely of varnished bamboo cane. The roof was supported by tall bamboo pillars, each topped by a carved golden dragon, its tail wrapped around the pillar, its outstretched limbs holding up the roof. "The Great Khan has had it so designed that it can be taken down and moved wherever he pleases," Marco wrote. "For it is held in place by more than 200 cords of silk."

Kublai spent the summer months at Shangdu, and the rest of the year at the magnificent new city he was building 200 miles to the southeast. The Mongols called the place Khanbalik, the City of the Khan. Kublai's Chinese subjects called it Daidu, the Great Capital, and it would grow into the modern capital of Beijing. The Khan invited the Polos to accompany him to Daidu, which was unlike any city Marco had ever seen.

"Planned with a degree of precision and beauty impossible to describe," Daidu was perfectly square and laid out like a chessboard, its broad streets a far cry from the narrow, twisting lanes of Venice. Boulevards leading to the imperial palace were wide enough for nine horsemen to gallop abreast. "The streets are so straight and wide," wrote Marco, "that the guards at one city gate can see all the way through the city to the guards at the opposite gate."

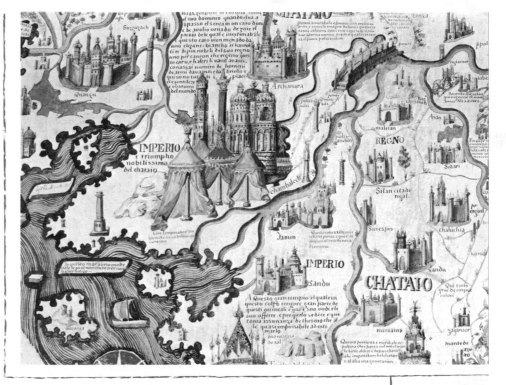

A detail of Kublai Khan's Daidu, present-day Beijing, from a reproduction of a 15th-century map of the world by Italian monk Fra Mauro. Mongolian architecture is depicted as distinctly European.

Daidu had many "fine homes and inns, with large courtyards and gardens. And along every main street there are booths and shops . . . offering more precious and costly wares than any other city in the world." Outside the city gates, more homes, shops, and hotels spilled over the landscape. "Actually," wrote Marco, "there are more people outside the walls in the outskirts than in the city itself."

What seemed like marvels to Europeans were, according to Marco, a normal part of everyday life in Mongol China. Homes were heated with "black stones that burn like logs." Marco had never seen coal, which was unknown in his part of Europe, so he was amazed that "these stones keep a fire going better than wood." Coal was so plentiful, in fact, that people could take hot baths every day, a custom that seemed astonishing, since in Europe, most people bathed rarely, and then mainly as a cure for gout or rheumatism. "Everyone goes to a bathhouse at least three times a week," Marco reported, "and in winter every day, if possible. And every man of means has a private bathroom in his house."

Marco was also impressed by China's efficient postal system. Ordinary messages were carried by foot-runners, who had relay stations three miles apart. Each runner wore a large belt hung with bells that announced his approach, so the next runner would be out on the road, waiting to take over. With these runners, a message could be delivered in just a day and a night over a distance that normally required a journey of several days.

Important messages were carried on horseback, with relay stations, called *yams*, spaced twenty-five or thirty miles apart along every main road. As the rider approached he sounded a horn. A fresh horse would be waiting for him, and he transferred to it and galloped on. "That is how these messengers are able to cover 250 miles a day," Marco explained. "When a message is urgent, they can cover 300 miles. . . . In such cases, they ride all night long. Messengers who can endure the fatigue of such a ride are highly prized."

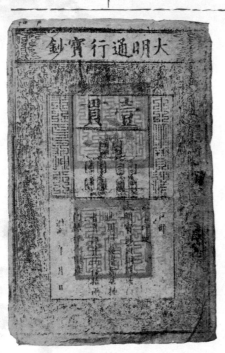

One of the first examples of Kublai Khan's paper money.

With Mongol relay stations extending out across the empire, this was the first truly international postal system. The *yams* also provided transport animals, guides, and comfortable overnight accommodations to merchants and other travelers.

But nothing in China amazed Marco more than the use of paper as a substitute for gold and silver coins. Paper itself was still largely unknown in Europe—documents and books were written on parchment, made from sheep- or goatskin. But paper *money* was something that seemed to defy common sense. The paper currency issued by the Khan was made from the pulverized bark of mulberry trees, and the larger the bill, the more it was worth. When bills had been circulating long enough to become worn, they could be turned in for fresh new bills. "You might say that the Great Khan has mastered the art of alchemy," wrote Marco, for he could print paper money that was as good as gold. "With these pieces of paper, people throughout the Khan's dominions can buy anything and pay for anything."

As the Khan's guests, the Polos were given apartments in the imperial palace at the heart of Daidu. Behind high walls guarded by Mongol warriors, the royal family occupied buildings and gardens "of great beauty and splendor." Here were the private quarters of the Mongol emperor himself, his four wives, his numerous concubines, and some of his forty-seven sons. Few foreigners, including Chinese, were allowed to enter the walled confines of this forbidden city.

A depiction of Kublai Khan, looking much like a European king, feasting, from the French *Li Livres du Grant Caam* (c. 1333), one of the earliest surviving Marco Polo illuminated manuscripts.

The palace dining hall, Marco reported, was large enough to seat 6,000 guests. At banquets, the Khan and his principal wife sat on an elevated platform, so he could look down and see everything. His sons and grandsons sat at a lower level, placed so that their heads were even with the Khan's feet. Lower down again were the knights and barons of the court and their ladies, with the remaining guests lower down still. Waiters who served the Khan on gold and silver dishes were specially selected knights and barons. "They have their mouths and noses covered by fine napkins of silk and gold, so that his food and drink are not tainted by human breath," Marco wrote.

On special occasions, such as a wedding or the Khan's birthday, the dining hall overflowed into the adjoining rooms, and the guests might number more than 40,000. Acrobats, contortionists, and jugglers performed, actors wearing masks danced and sang, and musicians played: "There are many musical instruments in the hall, and when the Great Khan is about to drink, they all strike up . . . all the guests fall to their knees and make a show of great humility, and then the Khan drinks. And each time he drinks, the whole ceremony is repeated."

Everything about Kublai Khan and his court was on a massive scale. He was attended by a personal guard of 12,000 barons and knights; by innumerable dukes, marquises, and counts; by astrologers, diviners, shamans, and physicians. At the beginning of the Mongol New Year, 5,000 gaily decorated elephants and "a vast number of camels" paraded before the Mongol ruler, each carrying a huge chest filled with gifts sent from all over his empire. By custom, he received nine times nine of everything—eighty-one bolts of fine silk, eighty-one pieces of gold, eighty-one pure white horses.

Every day, royal hunting parties went out to bring back food for the Khan's table and for his household of thousands. Some of these expeditions were led by the Khan himself. Too fat to ride a horse and suffering from gout, he rode stretched out on a silk couch covered with tiger skins in a gilded pavilion mounted on the backs of four elephants.

When he was ready to hunt, the roof of the pavilion rolled back to reveal the sky. At the Khan's signal, hundreds of falconers removed the leather hoods from their birds' heads. The peregrine falcons, gyrfalcons, and eagles took flight, racing after smaller birds and tearing them out of the sky, swooping down on ground prey and snatching them up, then returning with their kill to perch on the arms of their trainers. Some eagles were so large and powerful, they could catch wolves, deer, and wild goats by striking one claw into the prey's back and the other into its neck.

Huge mastiff dogs, sniffing and slobbering and straining at the leash, accompanied the hunting party. Tigers were carried along in cages on carts pulled by oxen, each tiger with a little dog for company, and were let loose when game was spotted. Leopards and lynxes rode on the hindquarters of horses, seated behind their trainers, waiting for the command to attack. Rows of archers stood ready to shoot any prey that could not be brought down by the hunting animals. And astrologers, diviners, and shamans rode out in front of the massive caravan, practicing their arts and clearing the path of clouds, rain, fog, or anything else that might spoil the Khan's hunt.

For all his power and wealth, the Khan, Marco tells us, was a just and humane ruler. In times of plenty he bought up crops, which he gave freely to the needy in times of famine or drought. He provided food and clothing for families "impoverished by some misfortune or disabled from working by illness. . . . No one who goes to his court in quest of bread is ever turned away empty-handed." Hospitals were established throughout the empire. And the Khan did not neglect the beauty of his realm, having tall trees planted along both sides of every main road.

Marco reported that homeless children were cared for and educated. While he says little about the system of education in China, we know from records of the time that Kublai Khan created thousands of public schools to provide a basic education for all children, including those of poor peasants. Until then, only the wealthy were literate. Kublai's bid at "universal education" had never been attempted by any country on Earth. In the western world, nearly 500 years would pass before governments began to take responsibility for the public education of all children.

But of all the Khan's policies and practices, it was his attitude toward religion that must have seemed the most remarkable to Europeans of the 13th century. Unlike the Christian kings of medieval Europe, where only a single religion was consistently tolerated, Kublai ruled over peoples of many faiths, among them Christians, Muslims, Buddhists, and Jews. While he demanded total loyalty from his conquered subjects, he decreed complete religious freedom throughout his empire in what was probably the first law of its kind anywhere in the world. Nowhere else could followers of so many different faiths worship side by side in peace. Outside the Mongol Empire, religious minorities were often persecuted, their sacred texts destroyed, their faithful believers driven out of cities and towns and sometimes burned alive.

Like his grandfather Genghis Khan and his Mongol ancestors, Kublai Khan worshipped the Eternal Blue Sky, the Golden Light of the Sun, and the innumerable spiritual forces of

nature. He also celebrated Christmas and Easter and observed the holidays and feasts of Muslims, Buddhists, and Jews. "I'll respect them all," he told Marco Polo. "The Mongols do not care which god is worshipped in their lands," Marco wrote. "If only all are faithful to the Great Khan and obey his laws, they may do whatever they please with their souls."

While Kublai ruled over a vast empire, he never forgot the simpler life of his nomadic ancestors, who lived in large round tents called *yurts* and moved from place to place according to the seasons. In the courtyard of his palace, he sowed seeds of prairie grass — a reminder of the Mongolian steppes and the freer world from which he had come.

"The people hold him in such esteem, that they revere him as a god," wrote Marco. "Let me add one more fact, and a very remarkable one. On certain occasions a great lion is led into the Great Khan's presence, and as soon as it sees him, it flings itself down before him with every sign of veneration, and seems to acknowledge him as its lord. And there it remains lying at his feet, entirely unchained. Truly this must seem a strange story to those who have not seen such a thing!"

The City of Heaven

We are told that Marco was quick to learn the customs of the Mongols, that he came to speak several languages, and that "the Khan held him in great esteem." He soon rose to a high position in Kublai Khan's court.

Kublai had not yet subdued the last of the southern Chinese provinces that had held out against his armies. As the foreign ruler of a conquered land, he did not entirely trust Chinese officials, who regarded him as a barbarian and resented his rule. Rather than rely on the Chinese, Kublai hired thousands of Persians, Arabs, and other foreigners as officials and administrators. Seeing that Marco had "so much sense, and conducted himself so well," the Khan employed him as a trusted envoy and sent him on "confidential missions to every part of the empire."

Marco had noticed that when the Khan's envoys returned from a mission, they reported on the business they had undertaken but had little to say about daily life in the places they had visited. "Then the Khan would tell them that they were fools and ignoramuses," wrote Marco, "and that he would rather hear about the manners and customs of the countries they had seen, than simply be told of the business for which he had sent them—for he took great pleasure in hearing accounts of whatever was new to him."

And so Marco endeavored, wherever he went, to "learn about all kinds of different matters in the countries which he visited, in order to satisfy the curiosity of the Great Khan." In that way he became a special favorite of Khan's, who gave him the opportunity to explore

"more of the strange regions in this part of the world than any man who was ever born."

Marco traveled on horseback for months at a time, crossing China's many rivers on ferryboats, stopping to rest overnight at the *yams* spaced every twenty-five or thirty miles along the roads. He ventured as far as Tibet in the west and Burma (today's Myanmar) in the south, chronicling sights that no European had ever seen.

In the tropical rainforests of the Yunnan Province, he wrote, he encountered giant "snakes and serpents" that crawled about on squat legs and had jaws big enough to swallow a man: "They are so huge and hideous that they strike fear into anyone who sees them. . . . Some of these creatures have enormous heads, bulging eyes bigger than a loaf of bread, and great pointed teeth. They can swallow a person

A miniature showing the people and animals of the Yunnan Province, from the 15th-century British illuminated manuscript of Marco Polo's travels.

in one gulp. In short, they are so fierce-looking, so hideously ugly, that every man and beast must stand in fear and trembling of them."

Marco's "snakes and serpents" were evidently crocodiles, which didn't exist in Europe. "Let me tell you how these monsters are trapped," he wrote. Hunters planted razor-sharp knives along trails followed by the lumbering animals when they emerged from their dens at night. "When the creature comes down the trail to drink at a stream or lake, it runs into a knife with such force that the blade pierces its chest and rips its belly, and it dies on the spot. The hunters know that the animal is dead by the cawing of crows, and only then dare to approach their prey."

After killing one of these creatures, the hunters drew out the bile from its belly and sold it "for a high price, for it makes a powerful medicine." It seems that the crocodile's bile was regarded as a cure-all. Marco reported, "If a man is bitten by a mad dog, they give him a drop of this bile and he is cured in a moment. When a woman is hard in labor and cries aloud, she is given another such dose, and her baby is born right away. When someone is afflicted with a rash or any sort of growth, he applies a drop of this bile and is speedily cured."

In the rugged Yunnan mountains, Marco visited a hill tribe that he called the "Gold-teeth People," for they had "every tooth covered with gold." The men tattooed themselves, "making a stripe around their arms and legs with black dots. They take five needles joined together, and with these they prick their flesh until they draw blood, and then they rub in a certain black coloring stuff that produces an indelible stain. They consider it a distinction to ornament themselves in this way."

"The men are all gentlemen, according to their customs," Marco wrote. "They have no occupation but warfare, hunting, and falconry. All the work is done by the women." But when a baby was born, then the men gave their wives a break: "After one of the wives has given birth, she washes and swaddles the infant. Then her husband goes to bed with the baby by his side and lies in bed for forty days, while all his friends and relatives come to visit and entertain him. They do this, they say, because the woman has done her part by carrying the baby in her womb, and it's fair that the man should do his share."

The tribespeople believed that this practice helped establish a close bond between father and child. But while the man stayed in bed with the baby, receiving congratulations, his wife "does all the work of the house and waits upon her lord in bed."

Among the members of another tribe, men and women alike decorated themselves with

 37

elaborate tattoos: "They are covered all over with pictures of lions, dragons, birds, and whatnot. . . . They make these tattoos over their face and neck and chest, arms and hands, and belly, in short, over the whole body. And those who have the most of these decorations are the ones most admired."

While Marco offers detailed descriptions of places he visited and people he met, he says very little about his personal experiences. And on those rare occasions when he does write about himself, he seems, at times, to be boasting. According to one version of his book, Kublai Khan appointed Marco as governor of the important city of Yangzhou, where he ruled for three years. Scholars doubt this. They believe that Marco claimed to be more important than he really was. He was probably much too young to be appointed a governor, and in any case, no Chinese records have been found that mention Marco as an official. However, many records of that period have been lost or destroyed.

Another incident reported by Marco seems even less likely. He wrote that with his father and uncle, he took part in the Mongol siege of Xianjiang, the last city in southern China to surrender to the Khan's armies. The Polos, Marco tells us, supervised the construction of three powerful mangonels, or catapults — military engines used for hurling stones and other missiles at the walls of a besieged city. The resulting bombardment was so devastating, the city's citizens realized "that unless they surrendered, they were all dead men. So they made up their minds to surrender at all costs. . . . And the credit for this achievement was due to the good work of Niccolò, Maffeo, and Marco."

The problem with this story is that the siege of Xianjiang is known to have ended in 1273, two years before the Polos, according to Marco's own account, ever reached China.

Marco tells us that he spent most of his seventeen years in China in the east, the country's busiest and richest region. He traveled along tree-lined roads "thronged with merchants plying a profitable trade," riding past "well-tilled fields and vineyards." And he visited "splendid cities and fine towns, with thriving trade and industries," where pot-bellied officials shaded themselves beneath paper parasols and scholars argued over poetry. Wherever he went, he was impressed by the wealth and prosperity he saw.

China was a huge empire with a flourishing economy. People wore fine silk garments, ate their meals from beautiful porcelain dishes, purchased paperback books with paper currency, and lived in populous cities that no European town could match. Marco came to admire the people for "their excellent manners and their knowledge of many subjects, since they devote much time to study, and they treat their parents with great respect." And he comments often and with appreciation on "the great beauty and charm" of Chinese women.

Many of the cities that Marco visited were strung out along the Grand Canal, a transportation marvel that had no equal in Europe—and to this day remains the longest man-made waterway in the world. The canal

A 15th-century Indian illustration of a Chinese city under Mongol artillery attack.

stretched a thousand miles from the capital at Daidu to the southern city of Quinsai (today's Hangzhou). It teemed with ships and barges continually coming and going, carrying silk, spices, salt, grain, and all sorts of "merchandise of the greatest value."

Quinsai had been the capital of the Sung dynasty in southern China before surrendering to Kublai Khan's armies in 1276. The city's name meant "Capital," though Marco, who did not speak or read Chinese, wrote that "the name means 'City of Heaven.'" In his time, it was probably the world's largest city, many times bigger than his hometown, Venice. Located between a magnificent lake and a great river, Quinsai had broad streets and boulevards paved with brick and stone, and like Venice, an immense number of canals, making it as easy to get around by water as by land. Crossing the canals were thousands of brightly painted stone

A 15th-century French miniature of Quinsai from the Livre des Merveilles du Monde makes it look much like a European town.

bridges, many "with such lofty arches that big ships can pass under them, while over them pass carts and horses."

Marco's vivid description of Quinsai, its people, and their way of life is one of the high points of *The Description of the World*. If he can be believed, the citizens of that flourishing city in Mongol China enjoyed a standard of living unmatched by ordinary people anywhere in Europe. "It is without doubt the finest and most splendid city in the world," he wrote, "as I, Marco Polo, saw clearly with my own eyes."

An enormous amount of food was needed to feed a city the size of Quinsai. Venice had just one great central market. Marco was astounded to find that Quinsai had markets in ten main squares, each a half-mile long and a half-mile wide. On market days, forty to fifty thousand people visited each square, and judging from Marco's account, they were very picky about the food they bought: "There is always an abundant supply of meat and game of all kinds, such as deer and rabbits, partridge, pheasants, and quails, ducks, and geese . . . and a great variety of vegetables and fruits, above all, giant pears, weighing ten pounds apiece, and peaches in season, yellow and white, with a very delicate flavor." Pots of noodles bubbled over glowing coals. Live fish from river, sea, and lake, "plump and tasty," were displayed in wooden tanks. "So many fish are on sale, you would think it impossible that they could all be sold, and yet, in a few hours, the whole lot is cleared away, so great is the number of people who are accustomed to fine living. Indeed, they eat both fish and meat at the same meal."

Streets leading to the market squares were lined with "shops in which all sorts of crafts are practiced and every sort of luxury is on sale. In some shops, nothing is sold but spiced wine, which is being freshly made all the time and is very cheap. . . . Other streets are occupied by physicians and astrologers, who also teach reading and writing, and by many other professions. . . . At all hours, the crowds of people that you meet passing this way and that on their different errands is so great, no one would believe it possible that enough food could be found to fill so many mouths."

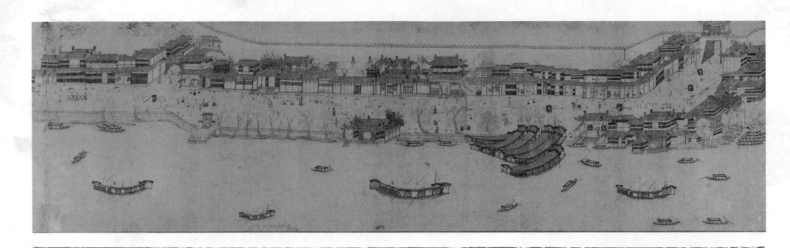

Marco reported that Quinsai had hundreds of public baths, "the most beautiful and largest and greatest baths that there are in the world. . . . There are many baths with cold water, staffed with attendants, male and female, who look after the men and women who go there for baths, for these people, from childhood on, are used to taking cold baths all the time, a habit they believe to be good for their health. It is their custom to wash every day, and they will not sit down to a meal without first washing. They also maintain in their bathhouses some rooms with hot water for the benefit of foreigners who, not being accustomed to cold water, can't stand it."

Along the shores of the lake at the edge of town stood "many handsome and spacious mansions, the homes of rich merchants and nobles." Out in the middle of the lake were two islands, each with a building "so luxurious it seems like an emperor's palace. When anyone wishes to celebrate a wedding or give a party, he goes to one of these palaces where everything is provided, such as crockery, napkins, table linens, and the like. It may happen that at one time, a hundred parties are going on at once, and they are all accommodated in different rooms and pavilions so efficiently that one does not get in the way of another."

Pleasure boats glided across the lake: "Anyone who likes to enjoy himself with his good friends hires one of these boats, which are completely furnished with tables and chairs and everything needed for a party. . . . On one side lies the city, so that the boat commands a distant view of all its grandeur and loveliness, its palaces, temples, monasteries, and gardens full of towering trees sloping down to the shore. And the lake is never without many such boats, for the people of this city, once they have finished the day's business, take great pleasure in passing the rest of the day with family and friends, either in these boats or driving about the city in horse-drawn carriages fitted with curtains and cushions of silk. They drive to public gardens, where they are entertained in pavilions built for that purpose, and there they divert themselves all the livelong day."

Was Marco exaggerating when he wrote that Quinsai had 12,000 stone bridges, 3,000 public baths, palace grounds ten miles in circumference, and 1,600,000 houses? Clearly, he was in love with the place and in awe of its pleasures and wealth. "When travelers return home," he wrote, "they say they have been to Quinsai, that is to say, the City of Heaven, and they can scarcely wait for a chance to return there."

As for Marco, he tells us that he returned many times.

Homeward Bound

The Polos were getting homesick, Marco wrote, and "they began to say among themselves that they would like to return to their own country." During their years in China, Niccolò and Maffeo had accumulated "great wealth in jewels and in gold," thanks to profits from trading and gifts from Kublai Khan. Kublai was in his seventies now, and his health was failing. If he should die, the Polos would lose their patron, their privileged standing at court, and perhaps their fortune. It was time to go home.

But Kublai wouldn't hear of it: "Time and again they asked the Khan to allow them to leave, but he was so fond of them and enjoyed their company so much that nothing on Earth would persuade him to let them go."

About this time, emissaries from Persia showed up at the Khan's court. They had come in search of a bride for their ruler, Arghun Khan, a great-nephew of Kublai Khan. To marry Arghun, Kublai chose a seventeen-year-old princess named Kokejin, a girl "of great beauty and charm." She was known as the Blue Princess, because her name meant that she was like the sky.

The emissaries set out for Persia with Kokejin, but they didn't get very far. Fighting had broken out among rival Mongol warlords along the caravan routes of Central Asia, making it too dangerous to continue. After eight months on the road, the princess and her escorts made their way back to Kublai's court.

Marco, as luck would have it, had just returned from "a voyage over strange seas"—a mission to the East Indies, perhaps. When he reported on his travels to the Khan, the Persians

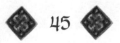

45

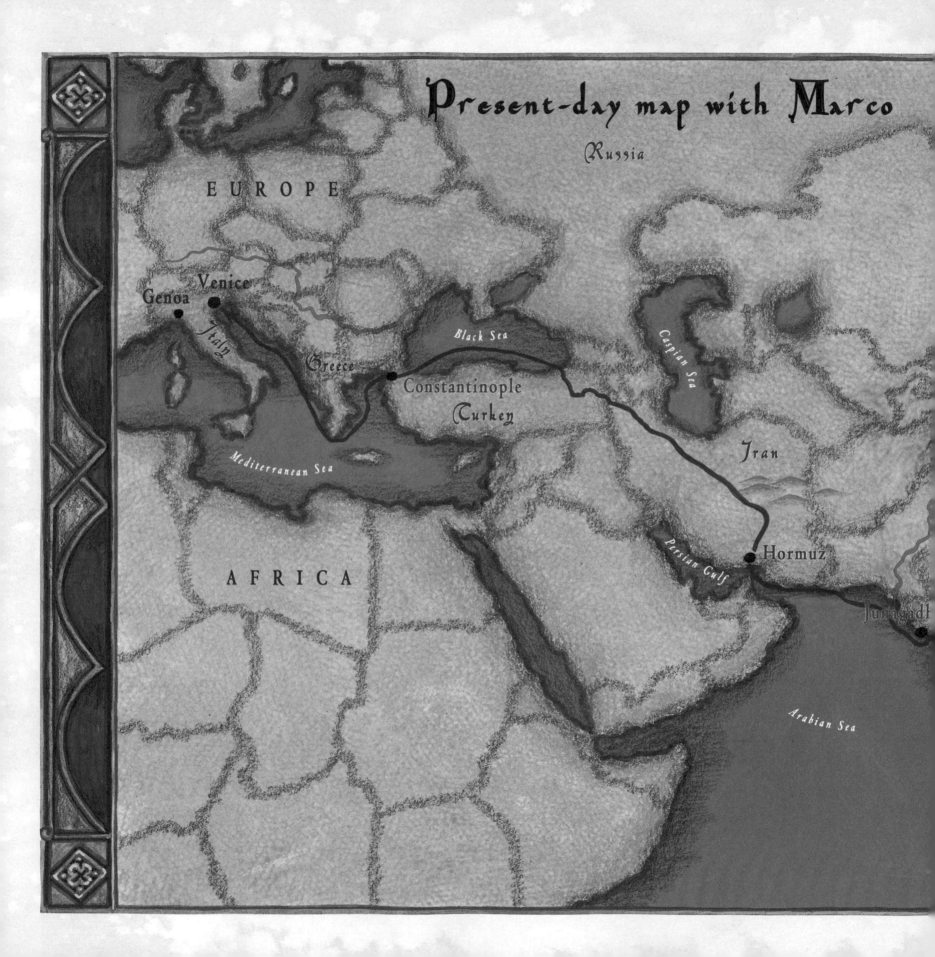

saw that he was an experienced and knowledgeable seaman. They decided that a sea voyage would be safer for the princess than an overland journey through a war zone, and they wanted Marco, Niccolò, and Maffeo to accompany them.

Kublai reluctantly granted permission for the Polos to leave. "His face showed great dissatisfaction," Marco reported. "If it hadn't been for the happy coincidence that led to our departure, we might never have gotten away and there is little likelihood that we would ever have returned to our own country." On the eve of their departure, Kublai gave the Polos two *paiza*, those hefty golden tablets that commanded officials throughout the Khan's realms to provide the travelers with everything they needed for their safety and comfort.

Kublai had ordered that a fleet of fourteen Chinese junks be outfitted for the voyage in the southern port city of Zaiton (today's Quanzhou). They were giant ships for the time, "as big as palaces," according to Marco, each with four masts carrying great sails of red silk stiffened by a series of bamboo slats, with oars that took four men to pull, and with as many as sixty passenger cabins. When the ships were ready, 600 passengers crowded aboard, among them the Polos, the Persian emissaries, and the Blue Princess with her attendants. Most of the other passengers were merchants on their way to India to buy exotic goods.

"There is much more that we could tell" about China, Marco wrote, "but the tale might become wearisome, so we will say no more." That's not the end of the story, however. They were about to sail to the islands of Sumatra and Ceylon (today's Sri Lanka), to the fabled kingdoms of India and beyond. Their homeward journey, Marco promised, would "offer many marvels unlike anything to be found in the rest of the world."

With bamboo-slat sails clattering in the breeze, the flotilla sailed into the South China Sea and along the coasts of present-day Vietnam and Malaysia. Marco says that they "sailed fully three months" before reaching the island of Sumatra, where the winds carrying them died. Then they "spent five months waiting for weather" that would permit them to continue their voyage.

Sumatra had eight kingdoms, each with its own ruler and language. The people along the coast were friendly and "traded with us for food and the like. There is plenty of fish to be had, the best in the world, and coconuts as big as a man's head, which are sweet and savory, and as white as milk." But the travelers heard that cannibals lived in the interior of the island, so they stayed close to the beach: "We disembarked from our ships and for fear of those nasty brutes who eat human flesh, we dug a big trench around our encampment . . . and built five wooden towers and we lived inside these fortifications."

When favorable winds returned, the Chinese junks continued their voyage, sailing west across the Bay of Bengal to the island of Ceylon, and from there to the southern coast of

The Polos and their fleet navigate Indian waters.

India, "where everything is different from what it is with us and excels in both size and beauty. They have no fruit the same as ours, no beast, no bird. This is because of the extreme heat."

The heat in southern India, Marco reported, "is so intense and the sun so powerful that it is scarcely tolerable. I assure you that if you put an egg into one of the rivers, you would not have to wait long before it boiled."

Like Sumatra, India was divided into several independent kingdoms. One king that Marco describes had "fully 500 wives" and thousands of royal attendants. He wore a necklace of "104 pearls and rubies of immense value," gold bracelets studded with precious stones around his arms, legs, and ankles, and "splendid pearls and other jewels on his toes." His only clothing in that hot and steamy climate was a "handsome loincloth with fringe all around it set with rubies, sapphires, and emeralds, a scrap of cloth that's worth a fortune."

The king's barons and knights "are his attendants in both this world and the next," Marco wrote. "Wherever the king goes, they keep him company. And when the king dies, and his body is burning on a huge funeral pyre, then all these barons and knights fling themselves into the fire and burn with him. For they say they have been his comrades in this world, and so they ought to keep him company in the next world."

Marco was fascinated by the Hindu holy men he met, who denied themselves worldly goods and comforts, slept naked on bare earth, and ate sparingly because they believed that all living things have souls. "They are called Yogis," he wrote. "I assure you that they would not kill any creature or any living thing, not even a fly, a flea, or a louse, or anything in fact that has life, because they say that all these have souls. For the same reason, they will not eat fresh vegetables, herbs, or roots until they have become dry, because while they are fresh, they too have souls."

Marco reported that India produced "most of the pearls and gems that are to be found in the world." He watched pearl divers "jump overboard from little boats and dive into the water, sometimes three fathoms down, sometimes four, sometimes as much as ten," as they collected oysters along the seabed all day. "They stay under as long as they can. When they can endure it no longer, they come to the surface, rest a short while, and then plunge in again."

Because the waters were infested with sharks, pearl merchants hired "enchanters," whose spells and incantations were meant to hypnotize the sharks and keep them at bay as the divers worked. "They utter their incantations by day only," Marco wrote. "At night they break off their spells, so that the sharks are free to do as they please." Did those spells really work?

Both merchants and divers must have thought so, because the enchanters, who were paid one pearl out of every twenty, continued to be employed for centuries.

India's riches attracted "merchants who come here in great numbers by sea and land." Junks from China and sailing ships called dhows from Persia and Arabia carrying valuable cargo crowded Indian ports. Offshore, pirate ships patroled the coastline, inflicting "great loss on the merchants." The pirates worked as teams, stationing themselves about five miles apart, so that twenty pirate ships covered 100 miles of sea. "As soon as they catch sight of a merchant ship," wrote Marco, "one signals to another by means of fire or smoke, so that no ship can pass through this region undetected."

Pearl diving, from the Bodleian Library's 15th-century British illuminated manuscript of Marco Polo's journey.

But the merchant ships were heavily armed and "defend themselves stoutly and inflict great damage on the attackers." Even so, some ships were captured. Then the pirates "help themselves to the cargo. But they do not harm the crew. They tell them, 'Go along with you and fetch another cargo. Then, with luck, you may give us some more.'"

Marco's fleet of Chinese junks had to sail through these pirate-infested waters as they cruised north along the Indian coast, then turned westward into the Arabian Sea. Marco doesn't say if they encountered pirates. In fact, he says very little about their voyage. And yet something awful must have befallen the fleet. According to one version of his book, only eighteen of the original 600 passengers survived.

What happened to the others? Were they lost at sea during storms or shipwrecks? Did they die from malaria, cholera, or some other fatal illness that travelers commonly faced in those days? We don't know what happened, or how many of the original fourteen vessels completed the voyage. Marco doesn't tell us. He does say that the Blue Princess was among the survivors.

At last, Marco's ship dropped anchor at Hormuz on the Persian Gulf, the city he had first seen as a teenager on his way to China. The 6,500-mile voyage from China had taken more than two years.

At Hormuz they learned that Arghun, the ruler that the princess was supposed to marry, had himself died. In keeping with Mongol custom, Kokejin was married instead to Arghun's son, Ghazan. Grateful to the Polos for delivering her safely, Ghazan rewarded them with four more gold *paiza* and assigned a cavalry escort to accompany them as they rode north across present-day Iran and Turkey. Kokejin had become deeply attached to the Polos, "and when

Rustichello and Marco Polo in their Genoese prison cell.

the three left her to go back to their own country, she wept with grief at their going."

Marco, Niccolò, and Maffeo returned to the domes and spires of Venice in the winter of 1295. They had been gone for nearly twenty-four years and had been given up for dead. Marco had left as a youth of seventeen. He came home as a man of forty-one. Niccolò and Maffeo were nearing seventy.

At first, no one recognized the homecoming travelers. Their clothing was shabby and worn after their long journey. They looked more like sunburned, weather-beaten Mongols from the northern steppes than citified Venetians, and they spoke with a strong Mongol accent. But they surprised everyone. Assembling their relatives, they ripped open the seams of their ragged garments and out fell a shower of rubies, diamonds, sapphires, and emeralds that they had sewn inside as a safeguard against bandits. With that, all of Venice "flocked to the house to embrace them," according to Giambattista Ramusio, a 16th-century Italian scholar who recorded the story of the Polos' homecoming as it had been passed down by family members.

Soon after the Polos returned, Marco found himself in the Genoese prison where he shared his "dungeon" with the writer Rustichello, who recorded the story of Marco's adventures as told by the great traveler himself. When Marco was released, he carried Rustichello's hand-written manuscript to Venice, where he apparently made changes and additions of his own. Meanwhile, scribes set to work with quills, copying and translating the book that came to be known as *The Description of the World* or *The Travels of Marco Polo.*

Marco spent the last twenty-five years of his life in his hometown. He married a Venetian noblewoman, raised three daughters, carried on a profitable trading business, and seems to have led a very dull and uneventful life compared to his adventurous past.

His book, meanwhile, took on a life of its own. "All Italy in a few months was full of it," wrote the scholar Ramusio. In an era when every book had to be copied by hand, *The Description of the World* circulated throughout Italy and was translated into several European languages. It became widely known by those privileged few who could read and by many others through word of mouth.

Even so, there were plenty of skeptics. They found it hard to believe that far to the East, beyond the endless steppes of Mongolia, there existed a hidden world they had known nothing about, a land of dazzling riches larger and more successful than their own.

To the end of his life, Marco resolutely defended the truth of his book. It is said that on his deathbed he murmured, "I have only told the half of what I saw."

He died, aged sixty-nine, on Sunday, January 8, 1324, between sunset and midnight, and was buried in the Church of San Lorenzo. Among his possessions were a gold *paiza* and the headdress of a Mongol princess, adorned with gold and pearls.

Did Marco Polo Go to China?

A German portrait of Marco Polo from the frontispiece of the 1477 Nuremberg edition of *The Description of the World*.

Marco Polo claimed to have traveled more widely than "any man since the Creation," and fact or fiction, his book made him famous. Scholars came to Venice to consult him on questions of geography. Scribes translated his book into Latin, Venetian, Tuscan, French, French-Italian, and German. By the time the first printed edition appeared in Nuremberg, Germany, in 1477, a century and a half after Marco's death, hundreds of handwritten manuscripts existed in most of the languages of western Europe.

Even so, people continued to question Marco's stories. Three centuries after his death, a British author, Sir Robert Burton, wondered if the chessboard-straight streets of Daidu and the 12,000 arched bridges of Quinsai really existed. In *The Anatomy of Melancholy* (1621), Burton imagines a journey by air where he will look down and discover once and for all "whether Marco Polo the Venetian's narration be true or false, of that great City of Quinsai and of [Daidu], whether there be any such places."

Despite lingering questions and doubts, Marco's book changed the way Europeans thought about the world beyond Europe. *The Description of the World* became the most influential source of information available at the time about China, India, and the East.

As Marco's place names began to show up on early European maps, other travelers were encouraged to set out for China themselves. Tombstones and documents show that during the 1300s, quite a few Italian merchants and missionaries followed the caravan routes to China. By 1325, a colony of Italian merchants resided at Zaiton (Quanzhou), the seaport from which the Polos and the Blue Princess had set sail nearly twenty-five years earlier.

But then the door to the East was slammed shut, following a Chinese rebellion that drove the Mongols back onto the steppes from which they had come. The triumphant Ming rulers of China expelled the Muslim, Christian, and Jewish traders whom the Mongols had encouraged, and they abolished many other Mongol policies. A century and a half would pass before China was again opened to foreigners.

During the 1400s, meanwhile, Marco's book seems to have fired the imagination of Christopher Columbus. He used his well-thumbed Latin translation as a guidebook, scribbling notes in the margins and underlining passages about gold, jewels, and spices, when he sailed west across the Atlantic, expecting to rediscover the land described by Marco Polo. When Columbus reached Cuba, he believed that he was at the edge of the Great Khan's realm and would soon find the Mongol kingdom of Cathay. Convinced that the lands of the Khan lay just a little farther to the north, in what is today the mainland of the United States, he decided that the people he met must be the Mongols' southern neighbors in India. And so Columbus called the native peoples of the Americas *Indians*, the name by which they have been known ever since.

Christopher Columbus, in a 1519 portrait by Italian painter Sebastiano del Piombo.

Today, Marco Polo stands unchallenged as the world's most famous traveler. And yet, after seven centuries, the truthfulness of his book is still being debated. How far can one trust what one reads in *The Description of the World*?

Some scholars suspect that neither Marco nor his father and uncle ever reached China. They argue that the Polos may have gone no farther than Constantinople (Istanbul) or the Black Sea, and that Marco simply collected tales told by Arab and Persian merchants who had actually been to China.

These skeptics question Marco's silence about many things in the China of his own era. Why, they ask, does he never mention the Great Wall? Why doesn't he say a single word about chopsticks or tea; about printing, which was invented in China; about Chinese script; or the custom of binding up young girls' feet? And if Marco really spent all that time in China, why doesn't his name appear in the imperial records?

Marco's defenders point out that the Great Wall as we know it today, with its sides and parapets built of brick and stone, wasn't all that great in Marco's time. That wall wasn't built until more than two centuries later. Marco may have seen the remains of a less impressive earthen wall, built 1400 years before he reached China. By the time he arrived, most of that original wall had fallen down.

A 13th-century Chinese portrait of the Great Khan.

Then why doesn't he mention chopsticks? As an aide to Kublai Khan, Marco spent much of his time with the Mongols, Persians, and other foreigners who made up the Khan's court. When eating with them, he probably used a knife to slice meat at the table, thereby disgusting the Chinese, who confined such acts to the kitchen. And he must have eaten everything else with his hands, rather than chopsticks, according to Mongol custom.

As for tea, Marco spent most of his time in North and Central China, where teahouses had not yet become common. And as a traveler from Italy, famous for its wines, he may not have had much interest in tea. He does mention, and often praises, many kinds of Chinese wines and spirits made from rice, wheat, grapes, plums, dates, and palm-tree sap.

Marco apparently spoke both Mongol and Turkish, and he

may have had some knowledge of Persian. He claims to have mastered a fourth language as well, but scholars have concluded that it wasn't Chinese. As a member of Kublai Khan's court, he probably spent little time with people who spoke Chinese. The Khan himself needed an interpreter when he spoke to his Chinese advisers. And Marco certainly couldn't read Chinese characters. This may explain why his book doesn't mention woodblock printing, an early Chinese invention, or the characters of Chinese calligraphy.

Another fact of life in medieval China ignored by Marco was the practice of binding the feet of young girls, a traditional status symbol for rich families. Women whose feet had been bound in childhood grew up with tiny feet that were considered elegant but made walking difficult. This practice was limited to upper-class Chinese women who were confined to their homes and would rarely be observed by anyone outside the family.

There may be other reasons as well why Marco's book doesn't mention these things. It's quite possible that he did write about them, but that those passages have been lost, along with his original manuscript. As scribes, and later printers, transcribed his book, working from earlier manuscripts and editions, they often added, subtracted, and mistranslated passages. That's why there are today some 150 versions of the book, no two exactly alike. And the original version, remember, was written down by Marco's fellow prisoner, Rustichello, who may have left out some of the stories Marco told, and who clearly added many touches and flourishes of his own.

Marco himself may have fiddled around with the text, adding, subtracting, and changing without the aid of Rustichello. Some scholars suspect that he wrote more than one version. His book includes descriptions of many places, such as Japan and Russia,

A 15th-century French miniature of a scribe at work. Illuminated manuscripts initially were the work of monasteries, but by the time Marco Polo's book appeared, they were also produced by studios of laypeople.

which he did not personally visit but only heard about from others; it includes stories about events he did not witness himself and people he did not personally meet, and at times, he mixes fable with fact.

What about Marco's claims that he served three years as governor of Yangzhou, and that the Polos played a key role in the siege of Xianjiang? Since these incidents are not mentioned at all in several versions of Marco's book, they can't necessarily be cited as evidence against his truthfulness. They may be exaggerations supplied by Rustichello to add drama to the story.

Finally, if Marco spent all that time in China, why doesn't his name appear in the imperial records? No Chinese record has been found that mentions him in any way. One possibility is that Marco, Niccolò, and Maffeo adopted Mongol names while they were living among the Mongol conquerers of China. And even then, many of the records concerning Kublai Khan's rule were destroyed after his dynasty was overthrown by revolts during the late 1300s.

Most of the scholars who have studied Marco's book regard it as essentially truthful. They doubt that he could have packed his account with so much detailed and precise information about life in China and the East if he hadn't been there in person and seen such things with his own eyes. Much of what he wrote was confirmed by later travelers who followed his Silk Road route and were amazed at how many details he got right.

Today, scholars around the world, and Chinese historians especially, continue to study the many versions of Marco's book in several languages. They regard *The Description of the World* as one of the most influential books of the Middle Ages, for it opened new vistas to the medieval mind and stirred the spirit of exploration. Fact or fancy, Marco's book affected the course of history and ended up not merely describing, but actually changing the map of the world.

Author's Note

The original manuscript of the book begun by Marco and Rustichello in their Genoese prison cell has been lost. The version thought to be the closest to Marco's original now belongs to the Bibliothèque Nationale de France in Paris, but that manuscript shows evident signs of abridgment.

All of the nearly 150 versions from medieval and Renaissance Europe include certain incidents and stories that seem questionable and may have been invented by Rustichello to add dramatic interest to the account. Also included are lengthy digressions on subjects that have little to do with Marco's personal experiences, such as legends of the Middle East and the history of the Mongols. And in all versions, Marco remains a rather shadowy, enigmatic figure, usually referred to in third person. His emphasis is on itemized descriptions of the world through which he traveled, rather than on anything he may have thought, felt, or did. His book is not a memoir or an autobiography, a genre that didn't become popular until centuries later.

The most prominent critic of Marco's credibility today is Frances Wood, head of the British Library's Chinese Department. In her book *Did Marco Polo Go to China?* (Boulder, CO: Westview Press, 1995), Wood examines Marco's many omissions and concludes that he probably never got beyond Persia, that he fabricated his story with the help of Arabs and Persians who had in fact visited China.

Wood's opinions are strenuously contested by historian John Larner of Glasgow University, Marco's most recent defender. In his book *Marco Polo and the Discovery of the World* (New Haven and London: Yale University Press, 1999), Larner reaffirms the overall authenticity of Marco's book, notwithstanding its exaggerations and inaccuracies. And he explores the book's influence on the history of geography and exploration, arguing that it played a key role in the development of European overseas expansion and European ideas about the rest of the world.

English translations of Marco's book are based on different versions of the manuscript, usually on more than one version, and consequently differ as much as the manuscripts themselves. Perhaps the most straightforward and readable translation for modern readers is R. E. Latham's *The Travels of Marco Polo* (London and New York: Penguin Books, 1958), which includes an informative introduction by the translator.

The recently reissued Yule-Cordier edition of *The Travels of Marco Polo* offers Henry Yule's annotated translation of 1871 as revised by Henri Cordier in 1903 (New York: Dover Publications, 1993). Reprinted in two volumes, this unabridged edition includes Yule's extensive editorial notations, which clarify and expand each chapter, along with some 170 woodcuts of Asia taken from Victorian contemporaries.

Other currently available translations include *The Travels of Marco Polo*, edited and revised from William Marsden's translation by Manuel Komroff, with an introduction by Jason Goodwin (New York: The Modern Library, 2001; Komroff's revised version was originally published in 1926). Marsden's original translation of 1818, as revised by Thomas Wright in 1854, has been reissued as *The Travels: Description of the World* (Cologne: Konemann Verglagsgellschaft, 1966).

Among the many latter-day adventurers who have attempted to follow in Marco Polo's footsteps, a writer-photographer team, Mike Edward and Michael Yamashita, reported on their adventures in three splendidly illustrated articles in *National Geographic* magazine for May, June, and July 2001.

Recently, it was estimated that anyone wanting to retrace Marco Polo's twenty-four-year odyssey today would have to travel 33,000 miles through seventeen countries and eight war zones, a trip requiring twenty visas (*paiza* not accepted).

And finally, it should be noted that no version of Marco's book claims that he brought pasta home from China and introduced it to Italy, as is widely believed. He didn't. Italy was already eating noodles. Another popular myth says that Marco saw ice creams being made in China, and on his return, introduced them to Italy, but this story too remains folklore rather than fact.

Equally mistaken are the beliefs that Marco brought back printing, gunpowder, and the compass (all Chinese inventions) to Europe. Among the items that he did in fact bring back were some yak wool, the dried head of a musk deer, and the seeds of various plants which failed to grow in the Venetian soil.

Art Note

Note on Bagram Ibatoulline's Art

Bagram Ibatoulline's style for the illustrations in this book changed to reflect the different cultures Marco Polo encountered on his historic journey. For the European portion of Marco's trip, Bagram was inspired by illuminated manuscripts, and drew from Christopher De Hamel's *A History of Illuminated Manuscripts* (Boston: David R. Godine, 1997) and Michelle P. Brown's *Understanding Illuminated Manuscripts: A Guide to Technical Terms* (Los Angeles: Getty Trust Publications, 1994). His portrait of Marco Polo on the title page is based on Enrico Podio's 19th-century mosaic portrait of the explorer, currently located in Genoa's Palazzo Tursi. For the Chinese portion of Marco's trip, Bagram consulted Annette Juliano's *Treasures of China* (New York: Richard Marek, 1981). His portrait of Kublai Khan on page 26 is influenced by Liu Kuan-Tao's 13th-century portrait, now in the National Palace Museum in Taipai, and his painting of Quinsai on page 34 is based on a late Ming Dynasty (1368-1644) drawing of Quinsai's West Lake.

Note on Archival Art

As translations of Marco Polo's *The Description of the World* appeared across Europe, French, English, German, and Spanish artists strove to illuminate marvels they'd never before imagined, and no other European eyes had seen. The results were sometimes peculiar—portly Kublai Khan appears in a French medieval manuscript as a slender king with distinctly European features. But European artists were not the first to attempt description of the wonders and the military might of the Mongols. Rashid al-Din, the great Persian historian and diplomat, supervised the creation of a richly illustrated history of the Mongols that was completed shortly after Marco returned home to Venice. And Marco Polo's account of his travels fueled the world's fascination with the powerful Mongol culture. Images from Marco's journey appeared around the world for centuries after he died, capturing the imagination of artists from the court of Akbar the Great in India, to Muslim miniaturists in far-off Persia, to Christian illuminated manuscript studios across

Europe. The different depictions in Europe and Asia of Marco's travels reflect a growing awareness of—and influence on—each other's cultures. As the art from cultures along Marco's path shows, the world was made both richer and smaller by his epic journey whether he took it or not.

Page 6: *The woodcut title page from the edition printed in Seville in 1503 of* The Description of the World. *The man on the left represents Marco Polo, the one on the right is Poggio Bracciolini, the author of the other text printed in the same volume; The Granger Collection, New York, New York.*

Page 10: *A French manuscript illumination of Niccolò and Maffeo Polo before the Great Khan, from the Livre des Merveilles du Monde (c.1410-12) by the workshop of the Boucicaut Master (c. 1412). There are only 138 surviving manuscripts of Marco Polo's travels, and only ten of those are illustrated, of which the Livre des Merveilles du Monde is one of the premier examples. Now in Paris, Bibliothèque Nationale de France, fr. 2810; akg-images, London.*

Page 11: *A 13th-century Persian illustration on vellum of Mongols laying siege to a citadel. Now in Paris, Bibliothèque Nationale de France; Bridgeman Art Library, New York, New York.*

Page 12: *A golden paiza from Mongol times;* Marco Polo, The Travels of Marco Polo, *vol. 2, trans. Henry Yule and Henri Cordier (London: J. Murray & New York, Scribner, 1903, reprinted in New York: Dover Publications, 1993), 353.*

Page 12: *A miniature from* Li Livres du Grant Caam *(c. 1410), an illuminated manuscript from England, painted on parchment with gold and silver leaf, of the Polos departing from Venice; copied from the British Library's illuminated manuscript of the same name. Now in Oxford, Bodleian Library, Bodley 264; The Granger Collection, New York, New York.*

Page 18: *The Catalan Atlas, thought to be the work of Cresques Abraham and produced in 1375, is the most highly regarded work to come out of Spain's Majorcan cartographic school. Painted on parchment with gold and silver leaf, the atlas includes astronomic and astrological charts, a tide table, as well as a map with Jerusalem at its center. Now in Berlin, Kuntsbibliothek at the Staatliche Museen. Art Resource, New York, New York.*

Page 21: *An engraving of camels traversing desert dunes by R. Long from a photograph by explorer Sven Hedin, believed to have been taken in the 19th century on a Central Asian expedition; Mary Evans Picture Library, London.*

Page 23: *Arriving at the court of Kublai Khan taken from the 1901 book* The Story of the Greatest Nations *by Edward Ellis and Charles Horne, (New York: F. R. Niglutsch Co.), contemporary hand-coloring; North Wind Picture Archive, Alfred, Maine.*

Page 26: *A 14th-century gouache illustration of Genghis Khan in battle, from the Persian School, taken from* The History of the Mongols *by Rashid-al-Din. Now in Paris, Bibliothèque Nationale de France; Bridgeman Art Library, New York, New York.*

Page 27: *A detail of Daidu and its surroundings from a reproduction of a world map created by Italian monk Fra Mauro with chartmaker Andrea Bianco, sometime between 1448 and 1453. Fra Mauro's map is one of the few that drew upon Marco Polo's descriptions of his travels. Now in Venice, Biblioteca Nazionale Marciana; Bridgeman Art Library, New York, New York.*

Page 28: *An illustration of Kublai Khan's paper money; from the 1903 volume,* The Book of Ser Marco Polo, *Henry Yule, (London: John Murray); Bridgeman Art Library, New York, New York.*

Page 29: *A miniature from* Li Livres du Grant Caam *(c. 1333), a French illuminated manuscript painted on parchment with gold and silver leaf, of Kublai Khan feasting. Now in London, British Library, Royal 19. D.i.; akg-images, London.*

Page 30: *A French manuscript illumination (c. 1412), painted on* parchment with gold and silver leaf, of Kublai Khan hunting from a pavilion atop four elephants, from the *Livre des Merveilles du Monde (c.1410-12)*, by the workshop of the Boucicaut Master. Now in Paris, Bibliothèque Nationale de France, fr. 2810; akg-images, London.

Page 32: *A 14th-century gouache illustration of Mongolian yurts from Rashid-al-Din's* The History of the Mongols. *Now in Paris, the Bibliothèque Nationale de France; Visioars / akg-images, London.*

Page 36: *A miniature from* Li Livres du Grant Caam *(c. 1410), an illuminated manuscript from England, painted on parchment with gold and silver leaf, of the people of the Yunnan, possibly showing the butchering of a crocodile in the upper left corner; copied from the British Library's illuminated manuscript of the same name. Now in Oxford, Bodleian Library, Bodley 264.*

Page 39: *An illustration (c. 1590) of Mongol warriors attacking a Chinese fortress from* The History of the Mongols, *originally from Lahore, Court of Akbar the Great. Now in Tehran, the library of Golestan Palace; Werner Forman / Art Resource, New York, New York.*

Page 40: *A miniature from the Livre des Merveilles du Monde (c.1410-12), a French illuminated manuscript painted on parchment with gold and silver leaf, depicting the roofs of Quinsai; from the workshop of the Boucicaut Master. Now in Paris, Bibliothèque Nationale de France, fr. 2810; Bridgeman Art Library, New York, New York.*

Page 42: *A 14th-century Chinese painting (handscroll, color on paper) of the pleasure boats of Quinsai, artist unknown; the Freer Gallery of Art, gift of Charles Lang Freer, F1911 209, detail, Smithsonian Institution, Washington, D.C.*

Page 48: *A miniature from the Livre des Merveilles du Monde (c.1410-12), a French illuminated manuscript painted on parchment with gold and silver leaf, of the Khan presenting a golden paiza to the Polos; from the workshop of the Boucicaut Master. Now in Paris, the Bibliothèque Nationale de France, fr. 2810; akg-images, London.*

Page 49: *The Polos' fleet in Indian waters; Marco Polo,* The Travels of Marco Polo, *vol. 2, trans. Henry Yule and Henri Cordier (London: J. Murray & New*

York: Scribner, 1903; reprinted in New York: Dover Publications, 1993), 248.

Page 51: *A miniature from* Li Livres du Grant Caam *(c. 1410), an illuminated manuscript from England, painted on parchment with gold and silver leaf, of pearl divers; copied from the British Library's illuminated manuscript of the same name. Now in Oxford, Bodleian Library, Bodley 264.*

Page 52: *Rustichello and Marco in their Genoese prison cell; Marco Polo,* The Travels of Marco Polo, *vol. 2, trans. Henry Yule and Henri Cordier (London: J. Murray & New York: Scribner, 1903; reprinted in New York: Dover Publications, 1993), xxxiv.*

Page 54: *A woodcut of Marco Polo from the Nuremberg edition of* Das Puch des Edln un Landtfareres Marcho Polo *(c. 1477, published by the House of Friedrich Creussner); there are eleven surviving copies, including the present one, with a hand-colored frontispiece. Now in New York, Columbia University, Rare Book and Manuscript Library; The Granger Collection, New York, New York.*

Page 55: *A 1519 portrait of Christopher Columbus (1446-1506) by Sebastiano del Piombo (1485-1574), an Italian painter of the Venetian school. The inscription naming the sitter as Christopher Columbus may not be original, but the portrait has become one of the most popular likenesses of Columbus. Now in New York, The Metropolitan Museum of Art; The Granger Collection, New York, New York.*

Page 56: *A 13th-century Chinese silk album leaf portrait of Kublai Khan, artist unknown. Now in Taipei, The National Palace Museum; The Granger Collection, New York, New York.*

Page 57: *A miniature from the* Histoire des Nobles Princes de Hainaut, *a 15th-century French illuminated manuscript on parchment, by Jacques de Guise. Now in Boulogne-sur-mer, Bibliothèque Municipale, France; Bridgeman Art Library, New York, New York.*

INDEX